SLOTHS

Slow Down and Sloth On
Calming Colouring Book

SLOTHS
Slow Down and Sloth On Calming Colouring Book

ISBN: 978-1-912511-13-6

Created by Christina Rose

Contributors: Frances Coles, Shutterstock

BELL & MACKENZIE
PUBLISHING LIMITED

www.bellmackenzie.com

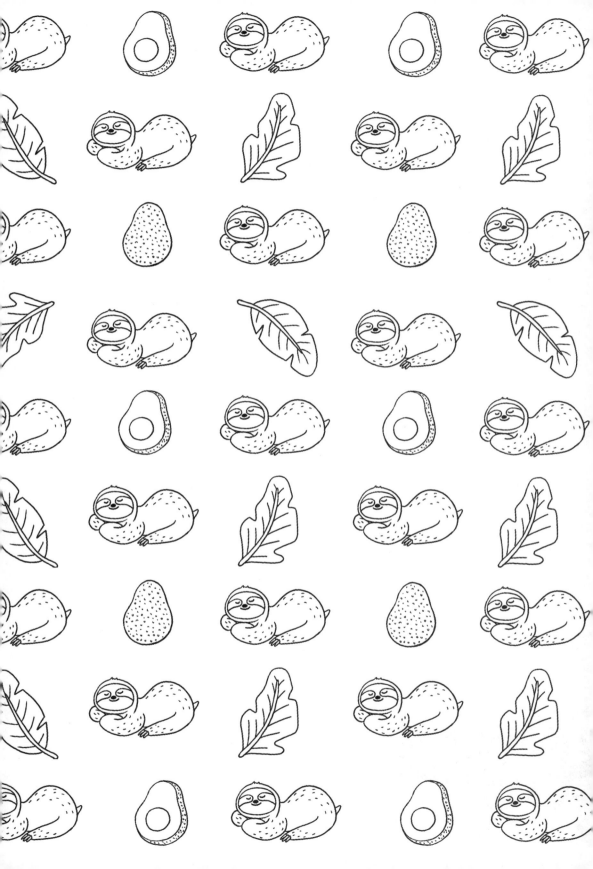

HUGS AND PRICKLES FOR FREE

YOU GET ME